Table of Contents

Introduction

Things to Keep In Mind About Running a Restaurant

Owning your own restaurant is among the most satisfying and fun business ventures. Food is a replenishable commodity. This implies that folks won't stop searching for various sources of food since dining out is amusing as well as functional.

Lots of people dream of running their very own restaurants, whether it is fast food, coffee shop or gourmet. Actually, lots of people fail to uphold their restaurants and the majority of them perish during their initial year of operation. This is because of the lack of groundwork and commitment on the part of the owner. Lots of people delve into the industry too quickly without really considering the pro's and con's of the venture or having the required expertise.

Nonetheless, there is a method to reduce the risk that is associated with new endeavors like restaurants. Preventive preparation and appropriate management are tricks towards success; however, there are also small things which matter in the entire process of running a restaurant.

Each business requires a business plan. Business plans are intended to set the various circumstances and characteristics that ought to be integral in the business. The accessibility of a great business plan which has been meticulously developed is a step towards excellence. You are going to find information about developing a business plan in a forthcoming chapter. However, certain points to think about are:

Clear-cut Description of the Idea of the Restaurant

The goal and the overall description of the idea of the restaurant must be specific. This is going to provide a general overview of what the restaurant aims to accomplish and for whom it plans to accomplish it. The idea of the restaurant needs to be set up because it is the main idea through which all else will follow.

There are numerous things to be taken into consideration in designing the entire idea of the restaurant (excluding food) like:

What kind of restaurant do you want?

What unique attributes would it have which might set it apart from all the other comparable restaurants in town?

What's the general selling variable of the restaurant?

Target Audience

The restaurant's target audience needs to be determined. No restaurant should attempt to pinpoint all types of people. Even fast-food restaurants have a particular target audience, although it may appear at first that it accommodates folks of all walks of life.

The idea of the restaurant needs to be lined up with the target audience. The target audience will depend upon the owner of the restaurant, and the options can be based upon the kind of food or even the individual taste of the owner.

Food Category, Food Items and Their Prices

Prior to launching a restaurant or even prior to entertaining the idea of launching a restaurant, the sort of food to be offered is typically identified first.

The majority of owners set up restaurants according to their favorite sort of food. There are likewise restaurants which are inspired by one-time experiences like eating outstanding international foods.

There are numerous options that are available for striving restaurant owners. The particulars of the food category ought to be determined next. The particular items in the menu ought to also be determined. Naturally, the pricing of these items is quite crucial for it will establish the feasibility of the business.

Financial Evaluation

After the prices of the food items have been established, it's time to create the financials of the venture. You can work with an expert consultant in figuring out the monetary viability of the restaurant. All the venture expenses and risks should be incorporated into the business plan.

Ownership

An enthusiast might think about establishing a small corporation or a partnership or a sole proprietorship to be in a position to grant the restaurant a legal entity. You ought to look at the local criteria for building such institutions.

There are numerous other things that ought to be taken into consideration before becoming part of the restaurant business. The ones noted above are just components of the entire scheme of restaurant creation. The most vital thing is that the restaurant should mirror the taste of the owner in order to make it pleasurable. Having said that, a lot of thought ought to be given to the way it's going to bring in cash because this is the only manner in which the restaurant will end up being sustainable.

We have addressed some of the vital information about possessing a business plan. This topic, along with other related planning information is addressed in depth in upcoming chapters.

Chapter 1: What Kind of Restaurant do You Want?

Different Kinds Of Restaurants

Entrepreneurs who are considering launching their own restaurants ought to recognize that restaurants are typically viewed as good business endeavors. Why? Because people are always searching for food.

There are various types of restaurants that entrepreneurs can consider starting up and the choice regarding what kind of restaurant or what design to put up is based upon various factors.

The choice regarding the overall idea of a restaurant business is going to hinge on different major things. Listed below are a few of these variables.

Location

The type of restaurant will hinge on the location. For instance, if somebody is considering putting up a Chinese-style restaurant in an area where there are numerous kinds of Chinese Restaurants, he might wish to fine-tune some details about his restaurant to be in a position to get a competitive advantage in opposition to the other Chinese restaurants in the location.

Maybe he would stick with the fundamental idea of owning a Chinese restaurant due to the fact that the place is well-known for this kind of food, but he might wish to include different kinds of food as well, perhaps go into fusion cooking.

Target Audience

The target audience is very essential in identifying what type of restaurant to put up. An active place where class B society flourishes may be an optimal area to set up a mid-scale fast food restaurant.

Various restaurants accommodate various kinds of folks and no one restaurant focuses on capturing the totality of the market since it would just wind up in confusion.

Accessibility of Materials

The budding restauranteur might wish to look carefully at the accessibility of the materials in the location. For instance, a seafood restaurant is going to depend significantly on the accessibility of fresh ingredients and seafood in the nearby market. Otherwise, the owner will need to look for other options which can cost him extra money.

Accessibility of good cooks

There are plenty of restaurants in lots of locations today. The only thing that differentiates the good ones from the standard is the kind of cooks. The type of restaurant ought to match the capabilities of the hired chef. There are excellent chefs who can quickly adapt to styles which they aren't truly suited for, but these chefs are extremely difficult to find, and maybe, they are going to ask for a really hefty salary.

Personal Preference

Naturally, each business is built upon a dream and the individual preference of the owner is going to determine the type of restaurant that he will launch. There are ways to defeat the typical odds which go against the prosperity of brand-new restaurants.

There are a great deal of various styles of restaurants which one can select from. These are:

Steakhouses

These restaurants typically accommodate the middle and upper class markets. These are likewise typically adapted towards families and have a very kicked back and homey environment. The meals in steakhouses are typically deemed as bargains. There are likewise the high-end steakhouses which focus more on the quality of the meat which they offer.

Seafood Restaurants

There are various kinds of seafood restaurants. There are the quick-service ones, the ones which accommodate the middle class and the higher-end ones which accommodate the upper class. The fast service seafood restaurants are quite comparable to fast-food restaurants. Typically, seafood restaurants provide a wide range of seafood and they offer it in various fashions.

Casual Dining

This kind of restaurant accommodates nearly all kinds of people. People go here to be in a position to have a bunch of food choices and delight in the relaxed kind of atmosphere. The prices in casual dining restaurants are typically not that substantial.

Pizzeria

There are generally two options in creating a pizzeria. The first one is to build a full-blown restaurant which doesn't just offer pizza but various types of Italian food as well. The other option is to focus on pizzas and a handful of other items like beer.

Coffeehouse

Increasingly more people are being tempted to go to coffeehouses. These coffeehouses provide the coziest environments for small talk and coffee chats.

These are just a few of the options that you have in creating an idea for your restaurant. Check out other options and stick with the one which pleases your heart the most.

Chapter 2: How are You Going to Design a Restaurant

A Great Design

A great design and layout plan are required for owning a good restaurant. Restaurants are excellent businesses which could be very satisfying. The simple fact that folks go to your restaurant to eat is actually something to treasure. It resembles having folks inside your house from time to time craving your home-baked goodies.

A successful restaurant is going to require a good design and layout plan. Design and layout plans hinge on various elements which are going to affect the final decisions later on.

As a matter of fact, the result of the layout plans can certainly impact the success of the restaurant. People frequently visit a new restaurant and they think to themselves "they should have put that plant somewhere else, it blocks the great view" or "I wish they hadn't set too much light in here." These are little things which can truly accumulate and wind up directing the customers to visit the opposite side of the street where another restaurant is calling out to their taste buds.

After the kind of food and service are determined, the following action is to work with consultants relating to the design of the restaurant. These are a number of the things that you want to take into account when thinking about various floor and layout plans for the restaurant.

Density of Customers

The layout plan ought to be based primarily on the convenience of the patrons. Even fast-food restaurants think about the density of folks, particularly in peak hours, although it may appear that these restaurants end up being too crowded during lunchtime.

For formal dining restaurants that accommodate the upper-class income, it might be a good idea to offer more room between the tables since these restaurants don't truly depend on the number of people per day. Their incomes rely on the pricing of the food items. There ought to be more provision for eye candy like furnishings and artworks.

Style of Service

The layout and floor plans should likewise be built upon the kind of service that the restaurant is going to offer. Fast food restaurants and self-service restaurants would require less space between the tables since the food won't be offered there. For additional restaurants which offer table service, the gap between the tables is truly vital so as to prevent excessive clutter from taking place in a specific portion of the restaurant.

Type of Building

The layout plan is limited by the kind of building where the restaurant is going to be built. You should have the ability to consider all the various curves and the minutiae in the structure before continuing.

Lighting

Appropriate lighting is really vital for each restaurant. The lighting should manage to complement the mood and the kind of service of the restaurant. A kicked back atmosphere may be enhanced by bright lighting while peaceful and serious moods might be accompanied by subtler shades.

Designing the restaurant is going to be split into two vital parts: the dining area and the production area.

The dining area is vital since this is the substance of the structure of the restaurant. The customers should be comfy in the restaurant and this is going to be identified as early as the developing phase. Studies have shown that half of the time, people arrive in restaurants as pairs, 30 percent arrive alone while the last 20 percent typically arrive in groups.

The production area is the next huge part of any restaurant. The important point about the production area ought to be efficiency. The organization of the kitchen is going to establish the rate by which the food can possibly be prepared and provided. The production area design should take into account other things such as room for storage, cooking, baking, garbage storage, production sections, staff facilities, etc.

In working with design consultants, the restaurant owner must, at all times, remember to place a clause of confidentiality in the contract. This is to stop the consultants from leaking particular aspects of the design to other individuals, particularly to the competitors. This can be as easy as a single-line clause which specifies that everything concerning the design is going to be owned by the client.

These are a number of useful things to keep in mind in designing your restaurant. The most vital thing to keep in mind are the folks who are going to be eating at the restaurant for they are going to be the lever of its success or downfall.

Chapter 3: Starting Costs to Take into Account

Understand Your Restaurant's Startup Cost

The expense of launching your own restaurant business is one very vital matter to be taken care of and frequently the toughest to figure out because, to a great extent, it hinges on the type of restaurant that you wish to open.

Your restaurant "start-up costs" are detailed as costs incurred for the acquisition or development of your restaurant business. "Start-up costs" are made up of any incurred amounts or out-going capital in relation with your restaurant's activity aimed at income generation prior to launching your restaurant business.

" Start-up costs" typically consist of the following expenses:

- Possible markets surveys.

- Assessment of available materials, labor, facilities, etc.

- Promotions.

- Business tools and fixtures

- Tool and fixture set up

- Designing and remodeling

- Employee outfits

- Wages for employees going through training and their coaches.

- Expenses of travel for obtaining prospective providers, distributors or patrons.

- Fees and salaries for specialists and executives and other comparable services.

Approximating your restaurant business' "start-up expenses":

It is a smart choice to examine your "start-up costs" approximation with a qualified accountant.

1. Start by recording, and then accumulate your whole restaurant's equipment which you regard as required to start and handle your restaurant.

2. On your list, check off particular things or equipment that aren't truly required and can wait.

Identify what sort of equipment needs to be purchased unused, and what kind can be bought used.

Identify what items might be leased, for the moment.

1. When aggregating the physical expense (building or office) of your restaurant, don't forget to include the remodeling expenses, decorating expenses, fixtures, setup and delivery fees for tools and fixtures.

2. Involve professional costs, utility deposits and permits.

3. When calculating your marketing expenses, ensure to add trademarks, logo costs in addition to other graphics to be utilized.

4. Think of ways where you might manage to reduce some costs. Call vendors and suppliers and work out particular bargains.

5. Estimate that all costs are going to be much greater than anticipated. It is reasonable to add about 1-5 percent to your estimation.

6. Compose your business plan before you arrive at your ultimate assessment

for "start-up expenses." Generally, a business plan operates to uncover more "start-up expenses" that weren't really considered.

7. Include your restaurant's first 3-6 months operating investment in your "start-up costs." These expenses will usually include employee salaries, advertising, rent, supplies, delivery expenses, utilities, taxes, insurance, maintenance, professional services, loan payments, inventory, etc

Before launching your restaurant:

1. Do work in or volunteer in a comparable restaurant such as the one you wish to launch. In doing this, you are going to have the ability to do menu formulation, restaurant marketing, payroll and numerous other vital aspects of the food business.

2. Identify your "target audience." What kind of crowd do you wish to serve? Is it teens, family or elderly people? Identifying your target customers before you start organizing will help you arrange your menu and is going to help set up your décor, ambiance, and the location of your business.

3. Select a food idea and style of service. Typically, your service style could be fast-food, serving fries, burgers, sandwiches and hotdogs; mid-scale serving value-priced complete "course dishes"; or upscale, offering high-class atmosphere with "full-service meals" with heftier prices.

4. Produce your business plan. See to it the plan consists of:

- Your restaurant's overall idea and goal;

- Comprehensive financial estimates and data; your food selection and pricing;

- Staff and tools details;

- Marketing and promotion plan;

- Feasible exit strategy.

5. Develop your menu. Understand that your menu can both "make or break" your dining establishment, therefore, it needs to be in accordance with your restaurant's entire concept.

6. Pick your location. Try to find a location where there is an ongoing stream of traffic, available parking, and close to or along other businesses.

7. Understand restaurant safety laws. Generally, restaurants are regulated and are subject to inspection. You need to understand the local laws and comply with them.

8. Hire your staff. Make sure that your job announcements particularly declare your specified demands.

Launching a restaurant business has its difficulties and, likewise, its rewards. Prior to launching any business, research first. Ensure you are fit for entrepreneurship in addition to recognizing that there is considerable effort needed.

Therefore, it is essential that you take pleasure in whatever you are venturing into in addition to you believing in your product or service since it will take the majority of your important time, particularly when you are starting out.

Chapter 4: Promoting the Restaurant

Advertising or Public Relations?

Favorable limelight is crucial for your restaurant's success; this acknowledgment can be achieved through "public relations campaign" in addition to advertising.

Note that a "public relations initiative" and advertising are two quite separate things. Both are suggested to raise the interest of customers in a product or service and both use typically the same resources, such as radio, tv, print and the internet, advertising utilizes ads and public relations utilizes news.

Here is a look at advertising and public relations differences:

1. Message management

Regarding how, where and when an advertisement circulates, is quite manageable. An ad space purchased in the appropriate format such as radio, broadcast, online, print, etc. suggests that you have control over the communications that you want to convey.

Meanwhile, while the message generation process via public relations is likewise very manageable, it is what takes place after your message has been sent that is typically unmanageable, which brings up the concern of whether prospective customers recognize the information you provided as newsworthy. Public relations ensure that is the case.

2. Information Personalization

Ads, being quite costly, don't give you ample room to tailor or personalize your restaurant's tale.

A public relations promotion carries this out, by producing a story of several angles aimed to successfully get to different media outlets such as daily papers, business journals, food service magazines, city publications, entertainment and eating publications, national magazines, etc. You boost your broadcast and connect with more audiences that are going to be informed about your restaurant.

3. Implied Endorsement

In advertising, you compensate someone to have your message specifically filtered to your possible consumers.

With public relations nonetheless, you can afford the dependability of an indirect endorsement of a "third-party." Implying you don't pay to get promoted, publications are provided to you for free, giving you room so you can depend on your restaurant's story to consumers. This endorsement is an efficient resource in shaping public opinion.

4.Cost-Effectiveness

There could be no comparison to the "expense" of display advertising in a magazine or publication as to the "expense" of circulating and composing an interesting press release.

Hiring a firm to produce press releases for your restaurant is certainly oftentimes cheaper compared to marketing expenses.

Additionally, press release articles are seen by more audiences since people are more curious about stories rather than advertisements.

5. Life Span

With public relations, a well-constructed story can have the interest of the audience for a long period of time, where an ad is seen by the visitor in a span of just 5 minutes.

Customers normally clip particular articles they check out, like a new destination that they would wish to go to or a new restaurant where they would wish to try the food.

The aim of public relations is to keep a "noise" or kind of a continuous talk about your restaurant and what it has to provide, and to develop trustworthiness. There are numerous media outlets that you can quickly get in touch with when you have developed a "well-expressed" plan in addition to the suitable public relations firm to execute it.

So when are you going to be utilizing public relations? Why and when to promote? The response lies with you and you alone. It all hinges on your requirements and on what you wish to achieve. You can use both marketing and public relations as your advertising instruments together, or individually as the situation demands.

Chapter 5: Market Research

Market Research

The food service market provides a universal requirement of humans which is to be fed. Having said that, the way food entices humans isn't in any way universal. Humanity is a diverse bunch and there isn't one specific operation of food service that might fulfill this diversity.

This is one truth which aspirants in the restaurant business find hard to acknowledge. Plenty of aspirants assume they can catch everybody, but such attempts wind up in failure. They forget to consider that attempting to accommodate everyone leads to not being able to satisfy anyone at all.

It is ideal to just focus on a small portion of the market, say ten percent or so, in this manner, you can provide the finest service for that aspect of your choice. This is accomplished by performing a market analysis, the research of the prospective target market.

The senior market is made up of folks who are 65 years or older. Elderly people typically live on fixed incomes, from their pension or nourishment by relatives, and therefore have rather stringent spending power. Most elderly people typically go to family-oriented restaurants like lunch buffets since they provide good food and services at inexpensive prices. Less active elderly people typically prefer tinier portions as they might have tinier appetites.

When pinpointing seniors, it is ideal to make them special by providing senior offers, or reduced rates. You can likewise promote your restaurant as senior-friendly by highlighting safety features like ramps and handlebars.

The late adult market is comprised of folks aged 50 to 64. They are typically the ones who are encountering empty nest syndrome, where adult children have left the house. This market typically has the most dependable financial standing as they might be in the most advanced phases in their careers. At this point, the price typically doesn't make a difference. This is the age when folks begin trying to enjoy life and its joys truly. So the primary consideration is good food and service. When targeting this market, it is great to provide your restaurant with style and elegance. It would be a good idea to spend more on ambiance and class.

The middle-aged bunch is made up of folks who are around 40 to 50 years old. These are quite productive years as most execs and standout career folks fall in this market. Money is quite abundant and thus spent with more charity. In this age, folks are quite keen on stylish and high-end, fine dining restaurants. Lots of people within this market actually have grandchildren and so this is likewise good for family-friendly restaurants which are more professional than those frequented by the elderly market.

The young adult market is composed of individuals in their mid-twenties to those that are just about to enter the middle age. This is an age of huge effort for established families. The primary worry here is appreciating children and maintaining a great relationship with them. Individuals belonging within this market typically look for eating places that contribute to connecting with their kids. Places that provide food quickly, and with larger quantities like family brunch buffet restaurants which are huge hits for this market. It is essential to offer convenience and a laid-back atmosphere for this kind of market.

The young market consists of those in their early twenties and younger. This is possibly the most diverse market. The primary consideration of folks in this market is instant gratification with affordable price. This is the main market for the fast-food sector. A good approach for this target audience is keeping up to date with the most recent trends and offering food services in accordance with what is "cool" and "hip."

Chapter 6: How Should You Accept Payments?

Possibly the most interesting part when setting up a restaurant, or any business for that matter, is gathering the cash. What is a business for but to generate cash? For some, the sole concern is the cash. Cash nowadays is no longer limited to a single financial form but various modes as well, which might be referred to as the three big C's-- cash, check, and card or charge. Which is the ideal form to earn? This might be a perplexing question for the aspiring entrepreneur. With any luck, the following is going to help clear things up.

Cash: Instant Gratification

Possibly the most frequent form of money is cash. Nothing whets the appetite for business such as crisp fresh bills. It is the monetary type you are most acquainted with and thus, the one most linked to profits and earnings. Cash is great since it is money in its purest form, concrete and tangible. It is instantly disposable and could be used anywhere.

Nonetheless, more people attempt to avoid holding cash nowadays. First, cash may be cumbersome; carrying a lot requires one to bring wads of paper. Second, considering that cash is tangible money, it is quite risky and might be lost. Once it is gone, there's virtually no way of getting it back. It can simply be stolen and can even draw danger by drawing in thieves and other bad elements. It can be hazardous to customers as they can simply be held up. It can be harmful to restaurateurs too because it can be quickly be embezzled. Although cash can provide instant gratification, great security is required to ensure its preservation.

Check: Symbolic Cash

Checks could be very handy for folks who have money in the bank. With checks, you may still spend money without needing to carry dense bundles of paper around. Checks can be rather safe as the money it exemplifies can only be claimed by the designated recipient, unless if the check is composed to be paid in cash.

There are numerous perks in using checks, but there are likewise drawbacks that might inconvenience the receiver. Checks need to be cashed, which requires time and extra work for the collector. The money gathered can't be spent right away. Checks expire after a couple of months, typically six. Perhaps the greatest harm that checks may involve are insufficient funds. The consumer paying with a check might not have ample money in their account.

Charge: A Guarantee to Be Redeemed

Plastic money or the credit card is now flourishing as the most prominent form of financial exchange. It is practical and easy to use. It is simple to carry and has a great deal of spending power in a tiny package. Customers love using it due to the extra benefits that come with it, like airline miles and reward gifts. On the recipient's end, money collection is guaranteed, considering that the responsibility of payment comes from the credit card firm, who carries the burden of going after delinquent customers as well. The payments might also be precisely credited to the recipient's bank account, making the sale risk-free.

Practical as it may be, credit cards aren't without drawbacks. Credit card firms usually charge considerable percentages of sales and might reduce your earnings. Money can also require time to collect and there is additional paperwork required to claim the money. Credit card scam is very feasible and can victimize both clients and restaurant owners.

Perhaps the ideal option of all is the debit card. The debit card stands for everything great about cash with none of the frustrations of checks. A debit card purchase resembles having immediate cash. A debit card resembles a credit card but operates as a check or cash. When a client presents a debit card, the vendor swipes the card similar to a credit card. The bank account of the presenter is queried to identify if there are enough funds in the account to pay for the purchase and the amount is instantly subtracted and moved to the merchant's account. This is certainly the next best thing to cash!

The Final Verdict

In selecting which mode of payment is ideal for one's restaurant, the ultimate choice comes down to the customer. Restaurateurs should bear in mind what mode is ideal for customers to pay, what is most hassle-free to them when it comes to their profile. It might not be recommended for a place that accommodates kids and teens to accept only credit cards considering that most youngsters don't have cards yet. It might not be recommended to reject checks or credit cards for fine dining that accommodates managers, as prices would be high. Obviously, it is great to have all the modes available.

With a meticulous study of the advantages of each mode of payment together with the market profile, an aspiring restaurateur may have the ability to select the finest payment option for their restaurant. Ideally, the money is going to rake in by the bundles, no matter if in cash, check, or charge.

Chapter 7: Creating Your Menu

The Craft of Menu Writing-- the Key to the Overall Success of Every Restaurant

Among the most regular fixtures in any good restaurant are the menus. They are among the initial things that greet you when you get in your favorite restaurant as they are typically posted at the entrance or instantly handed to you as soon as you are seated. You read them, utilize them, and then completely forget about them the moment the waiter has taken your order.

But menus accomplish more than just note what a restaurant can provide. The menu is crucial to the long-term success of the restaurant. Every little thing in a restaurant's operation is connected to the menu and is the reason that it is a really important matter to deal with when operating a restaurant. No matter how ordinary menus may appear to the layman, composing them properly requires effort.

The composition of the menu doesn't start with the actual writing of what the restaurant can provide, but begins way before that. The art of menu creation starts with the creation of the restaurant. At the restaurant's creation, a theme should be established and this theme ought to radiate through all the elements of the restaurant. Hodgepodge doesn't truly work, while fusion may.

Regardless if it is Italian, Japanese, Chinese, contemporary or homey, there ought to be a theme that will represent the personality of the restaurant. This theme is going to govern what is within the menu, from its initial print throughout all updates down the road. Having the theme helps shorten the menu, keeping it uncomplicated not just for the customer's eyes but also for the restaurant's stock. The motif will tell the owner or the chef what not to put in the menu and simultaneously, it will provide the chef an idea of what to incorporate.

After setting up the restaurant's theme and noting the possible items to feature in the menu, the following step is for the chef to jot down the recipes of the "candidate" products. Although the recipes seem not to concern the menu, it is highly connected as the procedures in the kitchen are set off by the customer's purchases, which are based upon the menu. The recipes are going to function as vital definitions of what is written on the menu. The recipes are essential to delivering the products in the menu as routinely as possible. If the chef can't convert the recipe of a specific item simply enough for the cooks to make it, then it is best to dispose of the item from the menu regardless of how good it might be. Only after the recipes have been documented can the menu be composed.

After composing the recipe and creating the menu draft, the following step is to get in touch with suppliers that supply the ingredients. The chef may be able to create recipes and a menu of delicious pieces, but they can't be created and offered if there are no ingredients. The chef and the owner ought to manage to source out the items diligently and thoroughly. It is best to get in touch with several suppliers to locate one that can provide the best quality, most consistent volume, and most sensible prices.

This phase in menu writing also establishes the prices of the food to be offered. The expenses of ingredients directly impact the price of the completed dishes. At this point, it might be required for the chef to replace certain ingredients that might be too costly to sell at a sensible price, or in worse instances, discard a dish completely because the expense might make it impossible to be offered.

When a bargain with suppliers has been ensured, the next vital step is to evaluate the menu. The chef has to put together the menu, and then introduce it to the entire restaurant, the busboys, the waiters, the managers, the owners, and anybody else included in the service. This is going to acquaint the entire restaurant to the food and additionally will help assess if the food is going to be good to serve. At this moment, it is wise to take photos of the dishes to work as a guide for the team so that they will understand how the finished dishes should look. At the end of the sampling, the chef will understand if there are required changes to be made in the menu. After which, the menu could be completed.

The final step will be the actual making of the menus. There are numerous menu suppliers that are going to be able to introduce several types of menus and components for the restaurant managers to select from. You may pick a booklet type of menu, or a single-paged one. The choices are endless. Restaurateurs might choose to contract out the printing of menus or they may choose to invest in a menu printer themselves should they consider it essential to change the menu more frequently than usual.

The menu might be merely a sheet of paper; nonetheless, it is an essential backbone of an effective restaurant. The steps to compose a menu may be tiresome, but the efforts to make one are certainly worth it.

Chapter 8: Choosing the Equipment and Furnishing

Very Helpful Tips on Furnishing Your Brand-new Restaurant

Lots of people dream of setting up their personal restaurant and succeeding on the culinary scene. Having said that, the majority of these dreamers stumble and slip since they don't know what it requires to have a good dining place. A good style, efficient team, and reasonable prices are typically planned. However, one vital thing may be neglected-- obtaining equipment and furnishings. Here are a number of valuable hints for equipping your restaurant.

The initial thing to do when searching for restaurant equipment is to understand what is required in a restaurant. The professional kitchen is so much more intricate than the one at home as food is made numerous times more than merely three meals a day. Developing a restaurant kitchen is quite crucial; you may consider employing an expert for this, however, if you don't have sufficient funds, you can still succeed by meticulously planning what to get.

As a basic rule, restaurant equipment and devices need to be straightforward, doing just what they are expected. Those with unique features more often than not have worthless functions that are just incorporated to increase their price. Complex machines also could result in complex breakdowns. You only require an oven that bakes, broils, or roasts, not so much one which shows you the time or buzzes when there is a thief. It is also ill-advised to purchase equipment that has mixed functions of typically separate machines. If one of the functions malfunctions, more likely, the other functions are going to do so as well, thus disabling your kitchen.

Obtaining restaurant equipment doesn't always imply buying. You typically have the choice to lease or rent equipment. Leasing is helpful for those who don't have sufficient finances to buy all equipment. Leasing also allows the owner purchase the equipment just when it is required to be used. The choice of getting better equipment is more reasonable with leasing; you can regularly get a new substitute piece after the lease of the former one ends.

Major upkeep of the equipment is likewise the obligation of the owner, which relieves you of the costs of repairing broken equipment. The downsides with leasing are that it might be rather costly in the long run, but in case you are making a lot, then its benefits might be worth it.

Some tools which are recommended to lease are coffeemakers, ice machines, dishwashers, and linens. Coffee machines could be acquired free of charge from companies that offer the coffee, as long as you keep purchasing your beans from them. Ice machines can wear out easily and it is recommended to lease them to avoid the hassle of continuous repairs. Dishwashers are rather expensive and leasing may be a great option to acquire them, and like with coffee firms, some detergent producers lend dishwashers to loyal consumers. Linens can likewise be leased, and typically, the lease consists of laundering, delivery, and storage.

New equipment could be quite costly, but who says you need to buy all brand-new equipment. There are numerous used restaurant equipment shops that might serve their purpose properly but cost numerous times less than new equipment. You just have to ensure that there is a guarantee from the seller that the devices will work, at least for some time. Disposable pieces like knobs and nuts are fine not to be in ideal condition since you can change them anyway.

What matters is the overall performance of the equipment. It should manage to work a sensible amount of time where you can continue to earn sufficiently at least to purchase new equipment when the old one eventually collapses. Among the equipment that is okay to purchase used are gas ranges, fryers, ovens, grills, and tools like tongs and mashers. They are typically straightforward tools that last long enough for a second owner to utilize decently.

Purchasing equipment is one of the most vital parts of creating a restaurant. With meticulous planning, you can make the most of your tools, with the most economical costs to you.

Chapter 10: How to Hire

Hiring the Finest Staff for Your Restaurant

The food service sector is one that includes a lot of personal relations. Hiring a great staff is among the most vital steps when launching your restaurant. It might make or break a restaurant, regardless of how good the atmosphere, the facilities, or the place. The recruitment process in a restaurant is very laborious, but thankfully, human resource practitioners have offered tips that can help in employing great restaurant staff.

The recruitment procedure for a restaurant doesn't begin with the actual interview and even the publishing of job ad. It starts with understanding what it is that the restaurant owner wants the staff to perform. Having a fundamental understanding of what tasks are needed of the crew helps produce the job summary which is essential for advertising the job openings and for sorting through the pool of candidates. The job description needs not to be too professional but it needs to state in a clear way the obligations of the position. They should also list essential needed credentials and abilities that the applicants should need to at least be taken into consideration.

The following thing to do is to develop a payment system. The services your prospective employees will provide you with should be remunerated accordingly. It is vital to look into the salary ranges in your area. For every position, you ought to set a range of salary since the pay also hinges on the workers. It is vital to fit the salary with the qualification of those you employ. Take into account the inclusion of tips for particular jobs.

It is also vital for you to develop an application form. Applicants should offer you the information you want to understand about them before you interview and employ them. Application forms ensure you receive the information you require for a clearer assessment of applicants and a better contrast with other potential employees. While resumes may offer more extensive looks on applicants, they may be short of specific information you may require to decide whether or not to employ someone.

The application form can likewise function as binding agreements for candidates to provide what they state to provide when you hire them. Application forms are designed for the precision of the information and you are able to utilize them to fire a person that doesn't produce as assured on the signed form. Application forms can additionally serve confirmation purposes to make sure that data from resumes is precise and consistent.

The interview is possibly the most vital part of the hiring procedure as it has the largest weight for your last decision. It is vital to understand that the interview might not be as precise in predicting the actual effectiveness of an employee as you may hope. There are candidates who shine in interviews with their communication skills and assurance but don't necessarily connect well with customers or remain loyal to you. Charisma can sway you and you ought to see through the shroud of charm. To accomplish this, you ought to ask questions that provide you with more unbiased information about the individual.

Ask about their hobbies and their backgrounds. Ask for certain occurrences that provide actual information about them. By the way, when they tell their experiences and hobbies, you may manage to see how they would connect with your consumers. Though hypothetical questions are going to give you a peek as to how imaginative the applicant may be, they aren't true indicators that you might use to anticipate the applicant's behavior accurately. You ought to also ask what the candidate's desires for the job are. This would reveal if the applicants recognize the line of work well enough for you to think about hiring them.

You shouldn't decide to hire immediately. Give yourself time after the interviews prior to offering the job to anybody. It is vital to consider all candidates and assess all their qualities and capabilities to come up with a decision. You should develop a short list of five people ranked depending on your inclination since you can't expect everybody to grab your offer instantly.

It is vital to hire a great staff for any restaurant. With meticulous planning of job demands and a payment scheme, plus a comprehensive selection of candidates, you are at least halfway to being an owner of an effective restaurant. Congrats!

Chapter 11: Business and a Financial Plan

Putting Together a Business and Financial Plan

The majority of wannabes of the restaurant business get thrilled with the hustle and bustle of the kitchen. Starting restaurant entrepreneurs strap themselves for the clashing and knocking of pots and pans and the activity on the restaurant floor. However, getting ready for the feats in a restaurant isn't sufficient, many who try to begin a restaurant fail to accomplish so since they overlook another vital, albeit less interesting part of the business, and that is the financial component. Many fail to recognize that a restaurant is, besides, a business, which necessitates careful planning. Here is a summary of how creating a business and financial plan is performed.

A restaurant's business and financial plan is typically made up of eleven parts that cover the forecasted operations.

1. Company Description. The business plan starts with an overview of the whole profile of the restaurant being created. This part explains what business entity will run the specific restaurant. The required information, like the company's founders and assets is the kind of information that is stated in this part. Supplementary information is additionally stated like the company's objectives and visions, the company's image, and so on. This part would also explain what kind of restaurant is being created, as well as its place, size, general target audience and other data that will provide the image of the restaurant.

2. Industry Research. This section offers a general overview of the restaurant sector. Careful research is required for this section in order to offer accurate numbers regarding previous trends as well as the forecasted performance of the sector. This section gives a reason as to why establishing the restaurant is a worthwhile endeavor.

3. Products and Services. This part explains what the restaurant will provide. Here, the fundamental theme of the menu is going to be described. This part will also provide the potential general development scheme, stating how the

food is going to be made and how other required measures in the production would be performed. The manner upon which the service is going to be delivered will be explained here too.

4. Market Research. This part describes the target audience. This will provide the profiles of the forecasted consumers, as well as the location where they are going to be coming from. This part will also feature a description of the noticed trends in the market, like the population growth, and additional factors that may impact the restaurant's operations.

5. Competition. This section explains the prospective competitors' profiles. Other restaurants throughout the area are going to be described. The specific restaurants that have an identical target audience will then be talked about furthermore. The intended competitive strategy is going to then be explained, stating how the intended restaurant is going to be different from the current ones.

6. Marketing Plans and Sales Approaches. This part of the plan is for ensuring that the restaurant flourishes. An overview of how the market is going to be penetrated will be presented here. This part will also specify the channels that will be utilized for marketing and creating awareness of the restaurant. The budget allocated for the marketing approach will also be specified.

7. Operations. This section is going to give the details of the operating system. This part will define the restaurant's facilities and tools. The hours of operation, in addition to the projected holidays, will be specified as well. The staff training and other parts of human resource management will be defined. The systems and controls, food creation, and other services will be clarified.

8. Management and Organization. This part will present the profiles of the managing division of the restaurant in addition to its ownership. The main employees and crucial managers will be identified here in addition to its board of directors. The compensation and incentive plan will be described. The management style and framework will be further explained.

9. Long Term Development and Exit Plans. This part will present the goals, approaches, and landmarks of the restaurant. This will also forecast opportunities for expansion. Risks will be assessed.

10. Financial Data and Projections. This part will present the current data about the company's resources at the start of the restaurant's development. It will additionally forecast projected numbers in sales, costs, profits and so forth.

11. Appendices. This is going to provide the actual data being explained in the body of the business plan. The actual menu, financial reports, declaration of resources and other vital information will be included here.

Owning a restaurant doesn't only involve work in the kitchen or on the floor. A restaurant is mainly a business, and the business part of its operations ought to also be focused on.

Chapter 12: To Borrow or Not to Borrow

Understanding When to Borrow Money or Get a Loan for Your New Business

There are numerous problems when it comes to money. In fact, there are lots of people and businesses that accommodate those in need of financial support. Borrowing money, nonetheless, may be complicated particularly with the stress of the conditions set forth by the rules of the contracts included. The trick is to understand when to borrow and who to borrow cash from.

There are numerous reasons why a person or a company turn to loans. A few of the reasons include:

- To begin their restaurant business

- For cash flow

- For business growth

Thus, the inspirations behind the act of borrowing money differ; and folks having these typical reasons for such loans have come to be target audiences for lending institutions.

Included beneath are sources of financial assistance:

- Banks.

- Credit Unions.

- Investors.

- Loved ones.

- Network of associations.

- Others.

The Do's of Borrowing Money

1. Do your analysis. Prior to borrowing money, ensure that the interest rate is within a sensible range.

2. Do compare. Choose the ideal banks that will provide you the ideal value for your money.

3. Do consolidate your borrowing actions to a single account. By doing this, handling your finances is going to be a whole lot simpler.

4. Do have a look at the contract. In case you are to sign for a loan, see to it that you manage to abide with the rules proposed by the conditions of the contract.

5. Do stay away from high-interest loans.

6. see to it that you are able to pay the loan to stay away from bad credit.

7. Do borrow in case it is of the highest necessity. See to it that you require the loan and that you are paying interest for a worthwhile venture.

8. Do keep an eye on the deadline of payments to stay away from service charges or fees.

Borrowing money may be daunting at first due to the risks involved. However, if you manage to invest the cash well and utilize it to make more money to pay your debt, then it ends up being a determined move with financial rewards. This is the reason that the business plan, marketing research and other actions we have covered are so essential.

Locating Investors

Funding your business might require you to make an application for a loan. Otherwise, you may choose an investor to finance your business instead. Drawing in investors may be accomplished with the use of a great business plan. After which, the issue is going to lie on finding investors who will be ready to invest.

There are numerous ways to search for investors; the simplest of which is via your personal associations. As a matter of fact, family members who are financially competent of investing are great people to start introducing your business plan. Furthermore, family friends or college buddies and colleagues trying to find ways to make a profit may have an interest in your business venture.

An additional way is to market. Locating investors with trustworthy backgrounds are of the highest importance. These prospective investors are also looking for promising business ideas, and they may very well be trying to find anything to invest in. Also, some have also managed to locate investors in this manner. Just see to it that your investor won't wind up stealing your business idea and start the business on their own.

Investors may, in some cases, offer more than financial assistance in guaranteeing the success of your business. This is particularly true when your investor focuses on the same field or market that your business accommodates. These investors understand the market very well via experience and may manage to give you prudent advice on how to operate the business. Additionally, as they invest their cash in your business, they will be quite interested in the condition of the business and with the return of their investment.

Borrowing money from any bank or any investor for that matter; calls for a high sense of accountability. It isn't something to be diminished and it should be followed with a proficient plan to guarantee payment of the loan or the return of investment.

Chapter 13: Location, Location, Location

Making the cut: Selecting the Ideal Location and Neighborhood for Your Restaurant Business

Setting up a business includes the mastery of the four P's of marketing: Product; Price; Place; and Promotion. Let's discuss the third P of marketing, which is trying to find a suitable "Place" or location for your new restaurant business. A badly situated business may very well imply the termination of the business; so its role in the success of the business is obvious.

Before selecting a location for your restaurant, it is vital that you are able to pinpoint the following factors:

- The kind of restaurant

- Target audience

- Budget designated for rent or purchase of space

- Facilities required in the set-up of the business

- Proximity of business location to your home

- Amount of room required to set-up the business

- Regional laws on property ownership, business licenses, and other laws that relate to establishing your business.

- Desired qualities of the space

- Company goals

- Others.

Assessing the requirements of the restaurant will serve to help you locate an appropriate location that will allow you to address those needs. Without a clear image of how the business is to operate and earn a profit; making smart and calculated decisions on issues such as picking a location will be close to inconceivable.

Surveying the Prospective Location of the Business.

A thorough evaluation of the neighborhood or community encompassing the location where you intend to set-up your restaurant is crucial in understanding if it is undoubtedly a match for your business. Keep in mind that your consumers will be coming from the local area, and it is essential that you have a sufficient amount of people inside the premises of your restaurant who are going to patronize your food services.

Discovering if the restaurant will flourish in a specific location is vital in guaranteeing the success of your business. To accomplish this, you need to do the following actions in surveying the neighborhood:

1. Perform a physical survey of the location. Spend time to see the folks in the area. Other factors like safety, tidiness, and so on may likewise be factored in.

2. Check out the competitors. Are there comparable businesses set up in the area? Find out the condition of their business.

3. Receive feedback from the folks in the community. You may provide surveys if you wish to evaluate the behavior of your target audience. By doing so, you are going to have an idea of how your restaurant might be seen if it is set up in that area.

4. Identify the spending activity of the target audience. It would be recommended to do a market research of the area where you plan to locate your restaurant. See the former chapter on Market Research.

5. Anticipate potential problems. If you choose to set up the business in the said place, will there be any issues down the road?

6. Find out the restrictions and constraints of the given area. Match your demands from the space required to put up your restaurant with what is offered and available with the given area or location. Are they a match?

7. Do the math! Identify the projected costs of establishing the restaurant in the intended location. Factor in the price of rent, tools, labor, and so forth.

8. Evaluate traffic flow and availability. Is the area accessible by foot or via transportation? It is vital to know how your market is going to manage to go to your location.

Depending on the features of your restaurant, the elements involving the choice to locate your business will likewise differ. Keep in mind that what may work for one kind of business may not benefit another. The reason being that not all businesses work alike and not all have the identical target audience. Thus, these variations need to be taken into consideration when making decisions relating to the restaurant business.

It really is all about locating that ideal match between your business requirements and with what a location is able to provide your business. Discovering the right location may not be simple but its importance to guaranteeing your business' success can't be overstated. Be patient and you'll soon discover the most appropriate area to house your business!

Concluding Chapter: Restaurant Business in the Long Run

Guaranteeing the Success of the Restaurant Industry's Long-term Future

In case you own a restaurant or you're considering operating one, then preparing for its long-term future is perhaps a big concern of yours. Much like any business, the restaurant industry has plenty of challenges and adjustments that influence of its' lifespan. To guarantee its continued success, a well thought out plan is absolutely a must!

The restaurant business requires market research before its set up and throughout its operations in the market. The said market research would typically tackle various elements in the target audience such as age, gender, line of work, income and education, to name a few. By determining these factors, the people operating the business will have an idea of ways in which to serve their consumers and prosper in competition with other restaurants accommodating the same target audience.

To carry out projections of the restaurant industry's long term future, it is vital first to evaluate the current condition of the business. In fact, there is a requirement to study its procedures and various circumstances as it advanced from "Day 1" to the present. And this can just be done through examining and updating the restaurant's business plan.

This is not to be mistaken with the business plan you developed when you were first embarking. A business plan should be revised frequently to guarantee that you are fulfilling your goals and targets. Having a frequently revised business plan is going to help you graph your progress and produce intelligent decisions concerning expansion or any other aspect of your business.

For starters, it is ideal to determine the various elements involved:

1. Business recap highlights

2. Company background

3. Research of marketing strategies throughout the years such as product, price, place, promotion

4. Comprehensive comparison of competitors

5. Comprehensive products and services provided and its evolution to what is offered at present

6. Sales approach and forecasts

7. Quality evaluation of management and procedures

8. Research of the financial plan, records of profits and loses, and so on

9. Others.

Change is continual, and to guarantee the long-term success of the restaurant industry, then alterations in various areas of society need to be factored in present circumstances and future projections. These are said to feature the changes in variables affecting the target audience and in whatever else that the business covers.

Furthermore, a business plan that deals with the long term future of the restaurant industry needs to be conceptualized.

A great restaurant business plan will include the following:
- Outline of the company's objectives.
- Competent knowledge of the company's niche.
- An organized plan that enables room for development.
- Changes and other societal conditions.
- Feasible and reasonable financial plan.
- Other relevant data.

Particular responses to the following questions need to be answered by the projections:

1. What are the market patterns in the restaurant industry?

2. How are these patterns altering?

3. What is the future market pattern projection based on population growth?

4. What are the anticipated attributes of the target audience in the long term future of the business?

5. How is the restaurant seen to develop with various adjustments in the market?

6. What are the product and service alterations anticipated in the future?

7. How have the rivals advanced?

8. What are the financial forecasts?

9. How will financial support be reinforced and sustained?

Various marketing approaches are going to help in guaranteeing the long term success of a restaurant. Numerous restaurants have actually urged the use of some of these marketing resources.

A.Use of In-Store marketing.

- Introducing of products.

- Promotional products and discounts in the store.

- Posters, leaflets, flyers.

- Restaurant style.

B.Use of Community Marketing.

- Community plans and charity work.

- Offers for locals.

- Sponsorship of neighborhood events.

C.Use of Media.

- Announcements in magazines and newspapers.

- Item features.

- Advertorials.

- Ads and commercials (if appropriate and within budget).

- Celebrity testimonials and/or customer testimonials.

- Brand visibility via sponsorship.

Besides the above-mentioned marketing approaches; it is vital to keep in mind that the quality of products and services must be preserved and cultivated. In fact, to guarantee long term success, there needs to exist a brand equity and a solid loyal consumer base.

To summarize the lengthy process; guaranteeing the long term future includes revising the business plan of the restaurant sector, review of products and services, brand growth, application of various marketing approaches, and so on.

Remaining in the restaurant industry may prove to be a very rewarding and gratifying experience. However, mismanagement and inept analysis of the market may also result in huge monetary losses. Thus, each step taken in this competitive sector must be thoroughly weighed and properly executed.